MEGA PICTURE PUZZLES

MEGA PICTURE PUZZLES
CHALLENGE YOURSELF TO SPOT THE DIFFERENCES

By What!Design

Ulysses
Press

Published in the U.S. by Ulysses Press
P.O. Box 3440
Berkeley, CA 94703
www.ulyssespress.com

ISBN10: 1-56975-645-7
ISBN13: 978-1-56975-645-4
Library of Congress Control Number 2007905470

Printed in the United States by Bang Printing

10 9 8 7 6 5 4 3 2 1

Design and production: what!design @ whatweb.com

Editorial: Nick Denton-Brown, Lauren Harrison, Elyce Petker, Abby Reser, Emma Silvers, Steven Zah Schwartz

Cover photos: © iStockphoto.com

Interior photos: © iStockphoto.com/Monika Adamczyk; Alvio; Leslie Banks; Carmen Martínez Banús; Diana Bier; Ben Blankenburg; Natalia Bratslavsky; Kjell Brynildsen; Dennis Guyitt; Lya Cattel; Norman Chan; Robert Churchill; Deejpilot; Diane Diederich; Jeremy Edwards; Elena Elisseeva; John Eklund; Steve Geer; Hedda Gjerpen; Gremlin; Sunny Gharaee; Richard Gunion; Alexander Hafemann; Ian Hamilton; Angel Manuel Herrero; Rainer Hillebrand; Nicholas Homrich; Timothy Hughes; Jaap2; InStock Photographic Ltd.; Michal Kram; Milan Klusacek; Yenwen Lu; Magui80; Georg Matzat; Vladimir Melnik; Nicholas Monu; Nixpixphoto; Christian Michael; Steven Miric; Pamela Moore; Skip Odonnell; James Pauls; PixHook; Toon Possemiers; Jack Puccio; Mirko Pernjakovic; Johan Ramberg; Giovanni Rinaldi; Michael Rolands; Simplesolutions; Dieter Spears; Eliza Snow; Devon Stephens; Martin Strmko; Terraxplorer; B Trenkel; Vasiliki Varvaki; Jacob Wackerhausen; Marcelo Wain; Serdar Yagci; YangYin; Zoubin Zarin

Distributed by Publishers Group West

CONTENTS

How to Use This Book

1 Spot the differences

Review both photos to spot the differences between them. Differences include color, size and removal or replacement of an object or part of an object.

2 Number of changes per puzzle

Each puzzle contains a list that shows the number of changes to it in order for you to keep score.

To check your results, see the complete list of puzzle solutions starting on page 164.

3 Level of complexity

The puzzle sections are divided into three levels of difficulty: Starter, Challenging and Advanced.

1 2 3 4 5 6 7 8 9 10 11 12 Score

Starter Puzzles

11

When looking for changes in the photo, watch for:

1 Changes in size or items moving

Items can change size or position in the photo. Some changes can be easy to miss. Look carefully for scale or position changes.

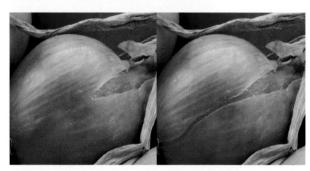

2 Items disappearing or changing shape

Did something disappear from the photo? Did it change shape?

3 Changes in color

Was that pumpkin orange or blue? Color can be very deceiving when you are looking at an everyday object. Be sure to review colors carefully.

4 But wait! There's more!

There are many ways of viewing an altered photo. In addition to the types of changes listed above, you will find other changes included to keep your brain busy.

STARTER

PUZZLES

Starter Puzzles

Happy Birthday!

1 2 3 4 5 6 7 8 9 10 11 Score

Taxi! Taxi!

Sushi Boat

CHALLENGING

PUZZLES

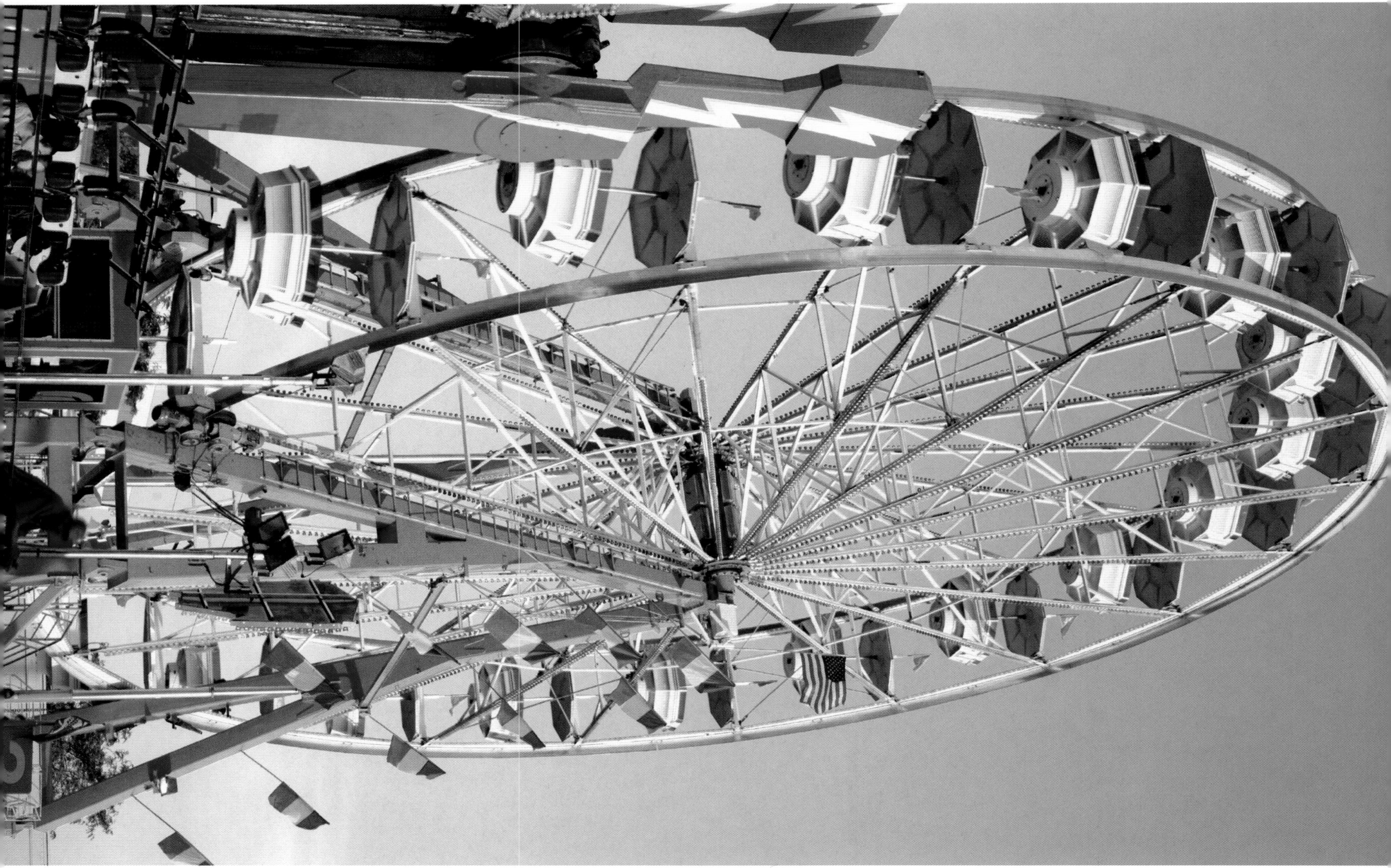

1 2 3 4 5 6 7 8 9 10 11 12 Score

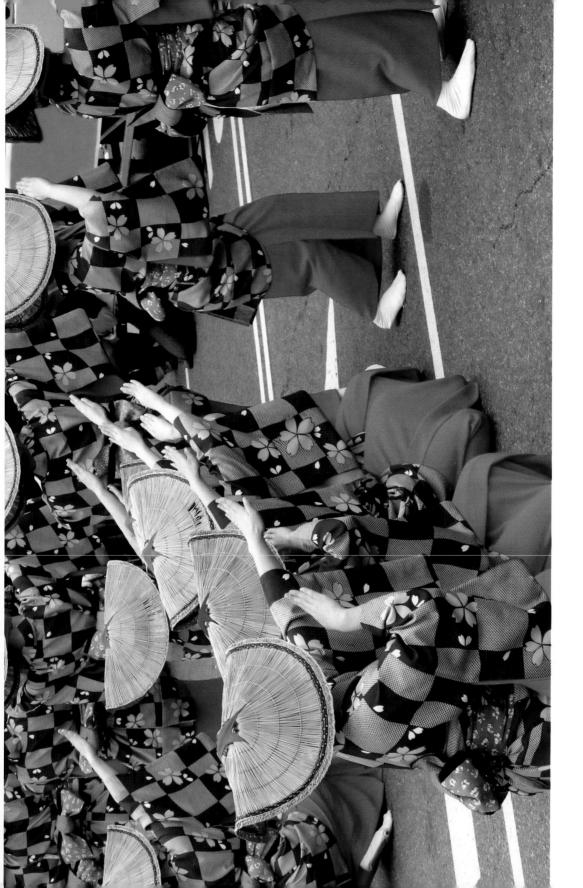

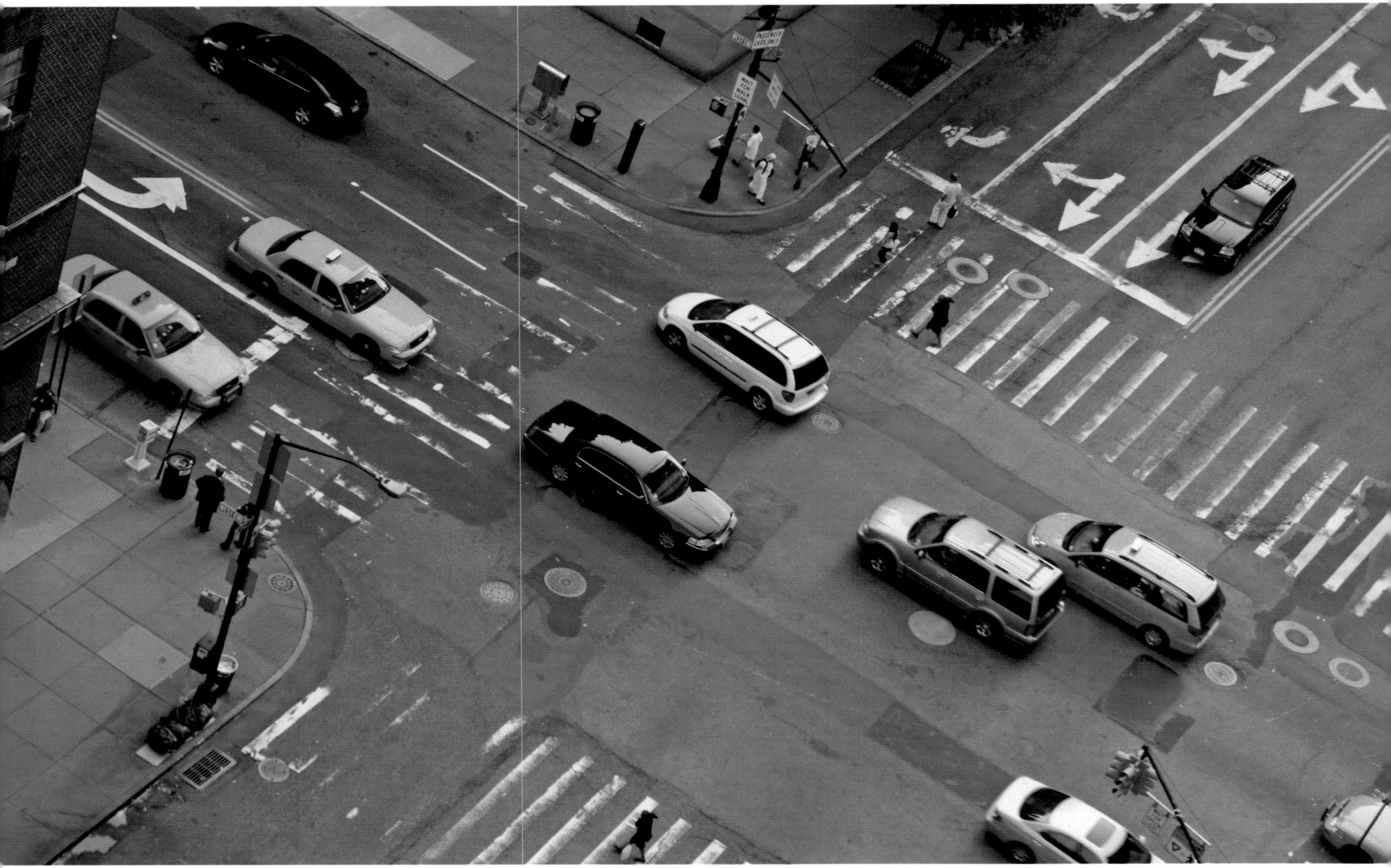

1 2 3 4 5 6 7 8 9 10 11 12 Score

Bookworm

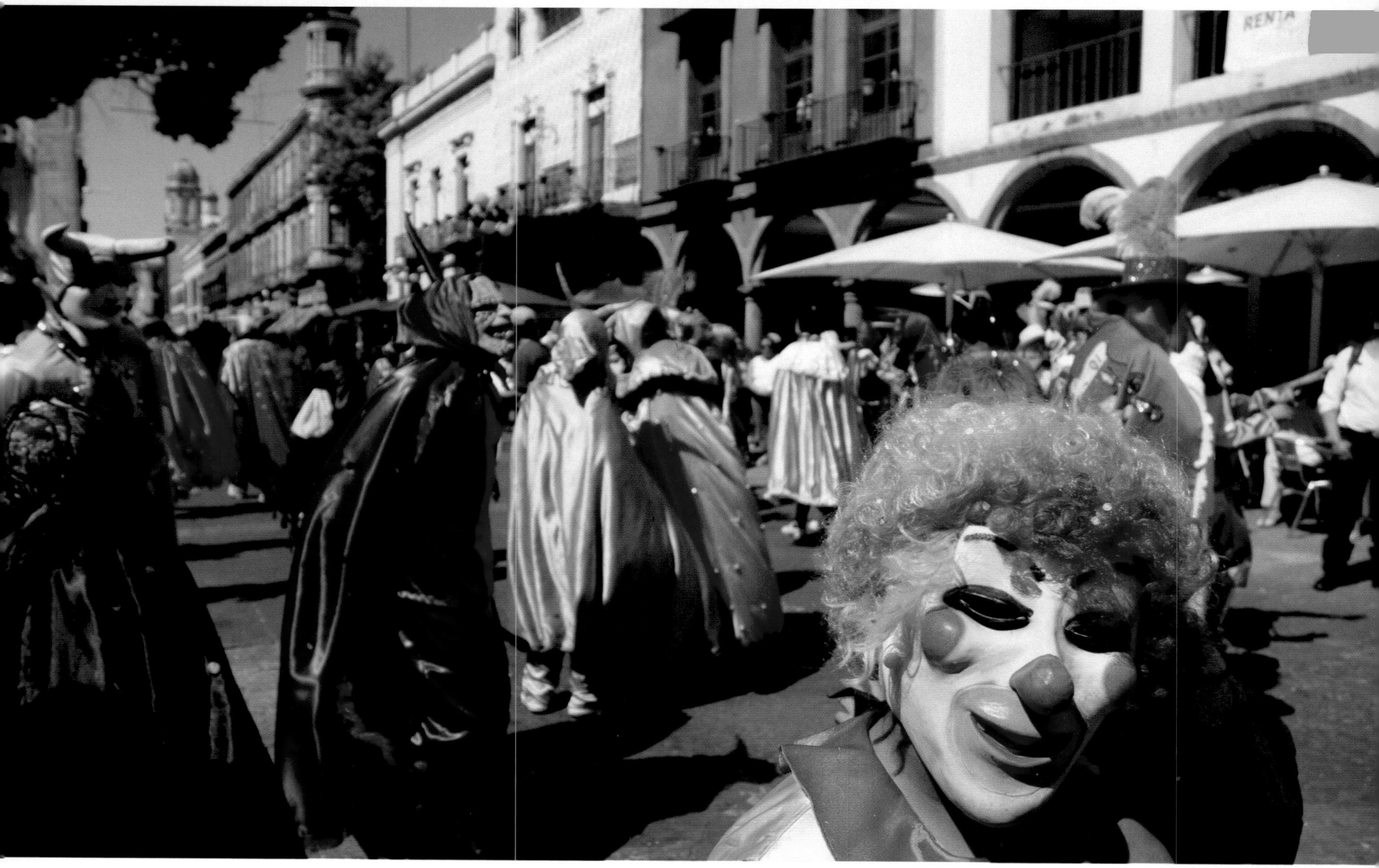

1 2 3 4 5 6 7 8 9 10 Score

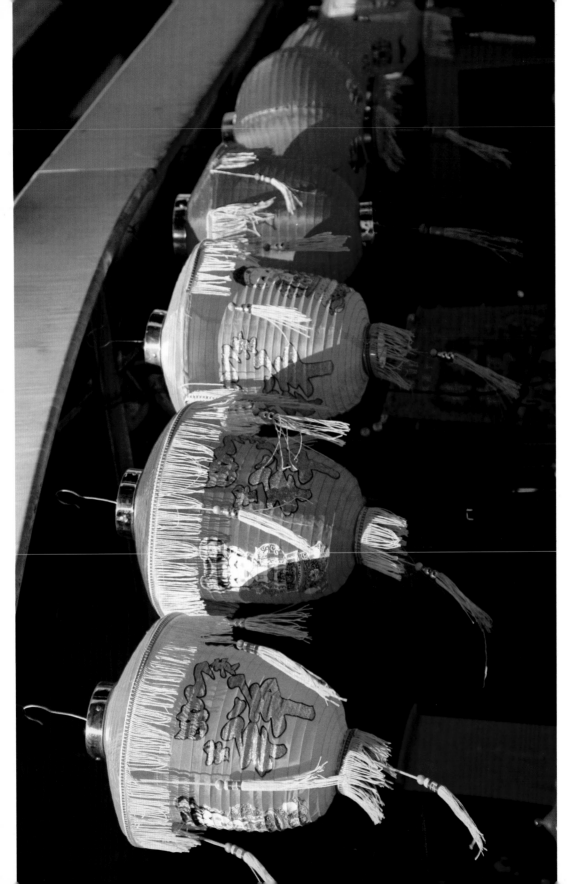

Garden of Changes

Mega Picture Puzzles

106

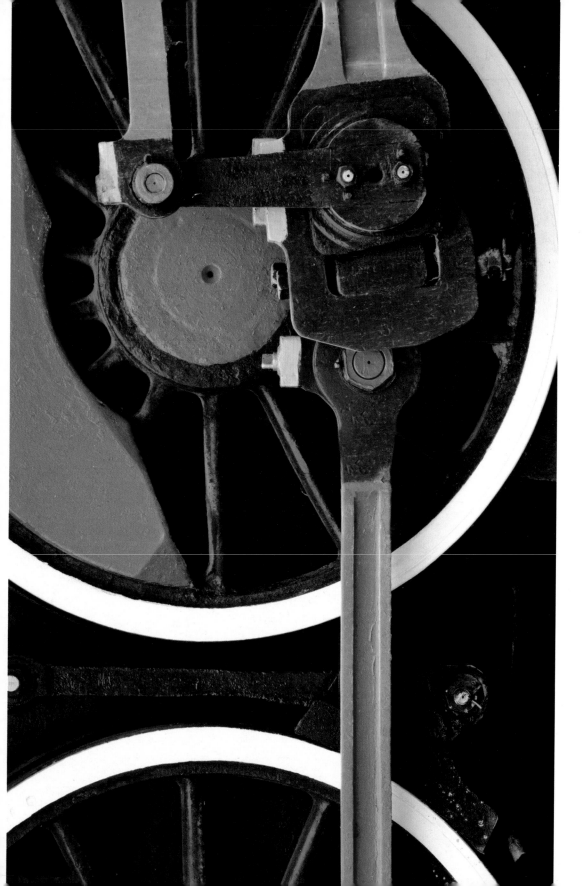

ADVANCED

PUZZLES

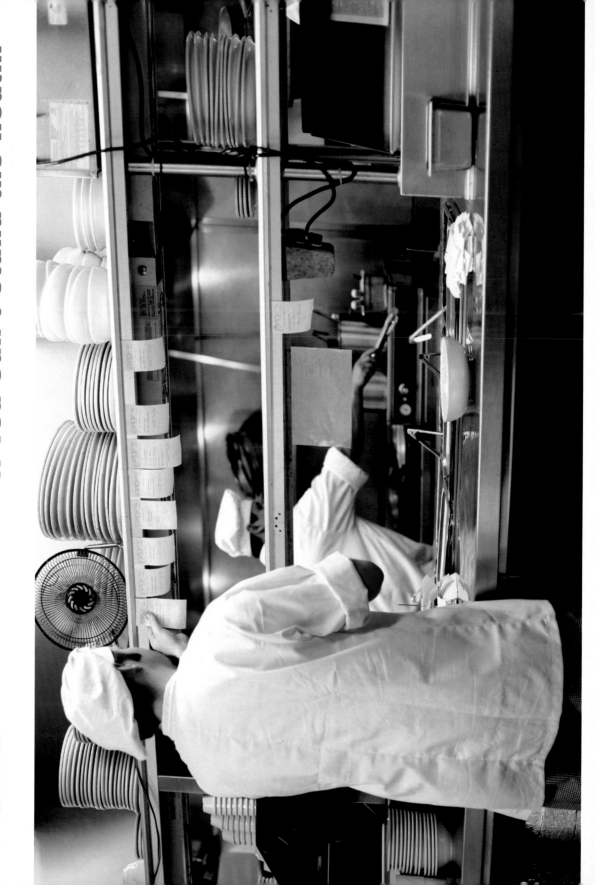

If You Can't Stand the Heat...

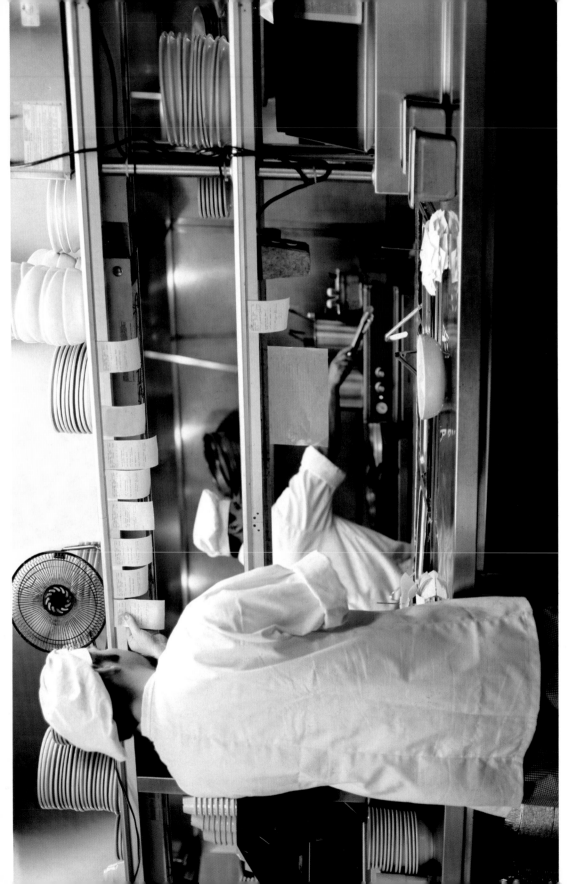

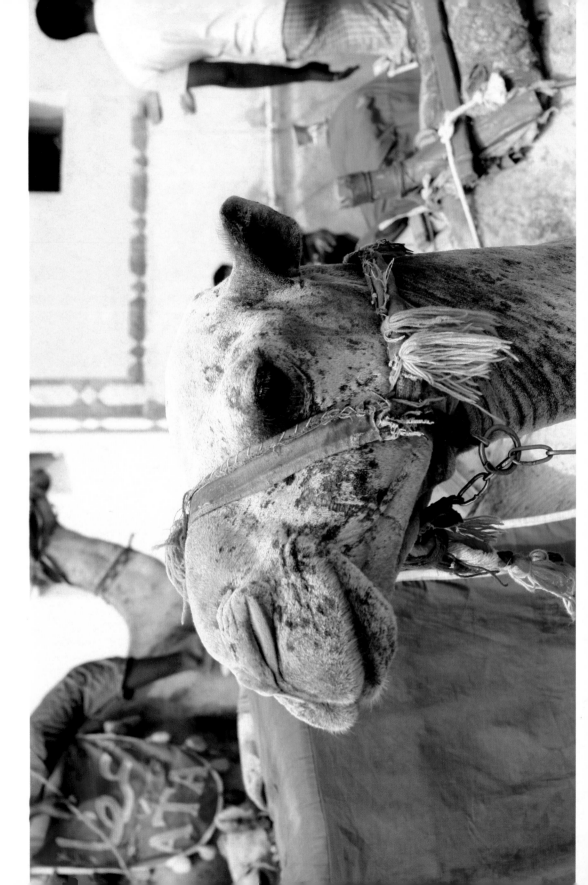

PUZZLE

SOLUTIONS

Page 10   **Harvest Time**

Page 12   **Happy Birthday!**

Page 14   **Uncorked**

Page 16   **Taxi! Taxi!**

Page 18   **Sushi Boat**

Page 20   **Busy Market**

Page 22   **Stop and Spot!**

Page 24   **Totem Town**

Page 26   **Fish Heads, Fish Heads**

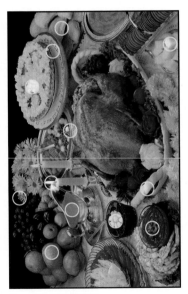

Page 28   **Bon Appétit!**

Page 32   Ships Ahoy!

Page 34   Let's Spice Things Up!

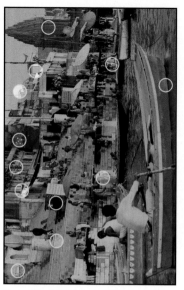

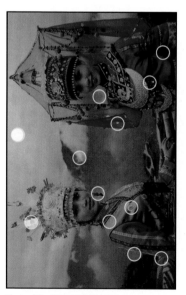

Page 48   3 2 1 Hike!

Page 50   I Love NYC

Page 52   English Telly

Page 54   What Happens in Vegas?

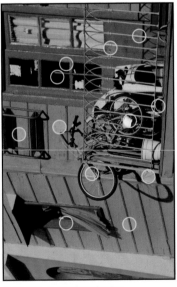

Page 56   Bright Sunshiny Day

Page 58   At the Country Fair

Page 60   Fresh Daily

Page 62   Dolls of the World

Page 64   Let's Party Like It's 1999

Page 66   Place Your Bets

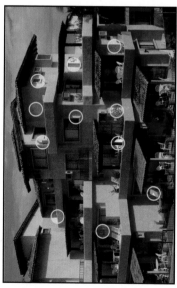

Page 68   Home in the Sun

Page 70   'Tis the Season

Page 72 The Neighborhood

Page 74 Citrus Blast

Page 76 At Old Town Square

Page 78 The Country Store

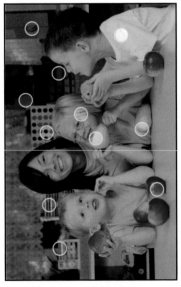

Page 80 Apples for the Teacher

Page 82 No More Homework,
No More Books

Page 84   Bookworm

Page 86   Farm Fresh

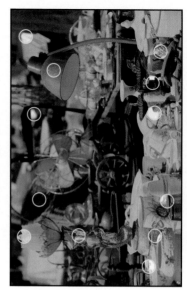

Page 88   Knickknacks

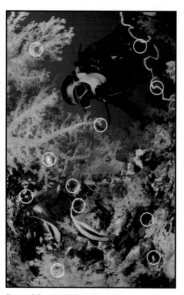

Page 90   Big Fish, Little Fish

Page 92   City of Water

Page 94   Clowning Around

Page 96   Land of the Dolls

Page 98   Family Vacation

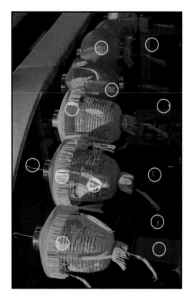

Page 100   Festive Scene

Page 102   Windows and Rooftops

Page 104   Antique Street

Page 106   Garden of Changes

Page 108   Nordic Neighborhood

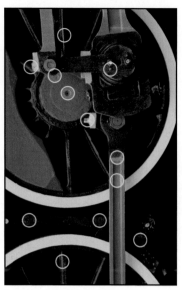

Page 110   Let Off Some Steam

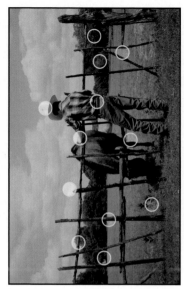

Page 112   On the Range

Page 114   Beautiful Afternoon

Page 116   Rustic Shelf

Page 118   Weather Report

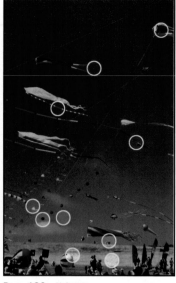

Page 120　Airborne

Page 122　Accordion Solo

Page 124　Catch the Brass Ring

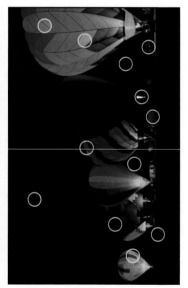

Page 126　Night Balloons

Page 128　Equestrian

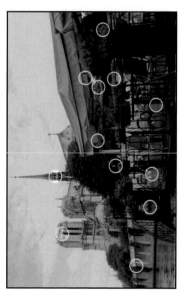

Page 130　On the Seine

Page 132   Flea Market Music

Page 134   Lunch Time

Page 136   Work Crew

Page 138   What's Cooking?

Page 142   English Study

Page 144   Shop Safety

Page 146   Study in Patterns

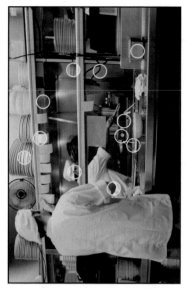

Page 148   If You Can't Stand the Heat...

Page 150   Drum Chief

Page 152   Nice Beadwork

Page 154   If I Had A Hammer

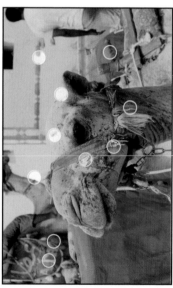

Page 156   Do the Humpty Hump

Page 158 **Endless Summer Days**

Page 160 **Let's Go to Chinatown**

About the Creator

Mega Picture Puzzles was designed and produced by the team at what!design, an award-winning design consultancy led by veteran creative director Damon Meibers, who co-founded the firm in 1998. Why create a puzzle book? The answer is more obvious than you may think — a love for problem solving. The book is a natural extension of what!design's work, as the firm solves puzzling design conundrums daily. But being good means nothing without doing good. The firm's passion for social justice has led them to collaborate with local and national non-profit organizations to raise awareness of social issues — and, naturally — to have fun.

what!design @ whatweb.com